SOLDIERS OF

To: John. R.N.L.I
Torquay. Doe?.

Regards.

Bernard Holles

The Author as a new recruit.

Soldiers of the Sea

by
Bernard Hallas

William Sessions Limited
York, England

© Bernard Hallas 2002

ISBN 1 85072 281 1

Printed in 11 on 12 point Plantin Typeface
from Author's Disk
by Sessions of York
The Ebor Press
York, England

CONTENTS

	Page
Byword	1
Messdeck Memories	2
Preface	3
Naval Terminology	4
In The Beginning	21
Spain	25
Dunkirk	27
The Stars	29
The Few	32
The Altmark	33
The 2nd Battle of Narvik	35
Murder at Sea	37
Convoys	39
Dawn Action Stations	42
The Malta Run	44
The African Campaign	46
Calabria	48
Taranto	50
Matapan	52
The Battle for Crete	56
The Royal Marines Battery	58
We Go East For Repairs	61
The Fall of Singapore	66
It Happened on a Sunday	69
The Rabble Comes Home	70
The Royal Marines Cutter Race	73
Salerno Harbour	78
Nelson's Blood (The Rum Ration)	82
The Old Lady	85
The Subject	86
At Peace With The World	88
What Is It?	89
The Thatcher Years	90
U.F.O's	93
Our Men of the Sea	92
Look Back in Anger	94

v

**The Royal Naval Prayer
of
Admiral of the Fleet**

**Lord Horatio Nelson
(at Trafalgar)
21st October 1805**

May the great God, whom I worship, grant to my country, and for the benefit of Europe in general, a great and glorious victory, and may no misconduct in anyone tarnish it, and may humanity after victory be the predominant feature of the British Fleet. For myself, individually, I commit my life to Him who made me, and may His blessing light upon my endeavours for serving my country faithfully. To Him I resign myself and the just cause which is entrusted to me to defend...

Amen,
Amen,
Amen.

Dedicated to my wife
Ruth
without whose help this
book would have been
impossible

BYWORD

The Author served for twelve years in
the Royal Marines from 1935 to 1947.
His wartime experiences were gained
on board Battleships and Cruisers –
especially H.M.S. Warspite the
Flagship of whichever Fleet she had
the privilege of serving in at the time.

He joined 'The Grand Old Lady' before
the outbreak of War and stayed with her
until she became inoperable after being hit
with a one thousand pound bomb during
the landings at Salerno in September 1943.

Most of the following narratives are
by-products of those very happy years
spent in very good company.

MESS DECK MEMORIES

Dedicated to those very special friends of mine, the Royal Marines of the Starboard 6" Battery of the Flagship of the Mediterranean Fleet H.M.S. Warspite, who died in action at 1320 hours on May 22nd 1941, in the battle for the island of Crete.

ROLL OF HONOUR

Arnold T.C.	CH/24566
Hadley W.	CH/X1894
Kent W.J.	CH/X3375
McKie J.R.	CH/X923
Meacock E.A.	CH/X424
Nichol W.H.	CH/X3321
Nunn F.T.	CH/X1952
Owen L.F.	CH/X2934
Ross P.	PL/X2152
Symons R.A.	CH/X3164

PREFACE

I have tried to tell my story
To take you back in time,
To explain the deeds of mortal men
And put it down in rhyme.

The whole of it is as near the truth
As memory will allow,
But thoughts grow dim as the years pass by
And most actors have taken their bow.

Those that remain will tell you
That not all of it was bad,
For out of it came friendships
No greater gift could be had.

Some that still live, may owe their lives
To others that did not return,
To them, we can only say "Thank You"
With the hope, that others may learn.

Bernard Hallas

INTRODUCTION TO ROYAL NAVY
TERMINOLOGY

To the ordinary "Land Lubber", that is a person who has never had the pleasure of serving at sea in any capacity not necessarily in the Armed Forces. Some of the sea going and dockside terminology may be a complete mystery.

I shall therefore try to explain the meaning of the ones in general use amongst the sea going fraternity.

First off, is the ship itself. We all know that a ship is always referred to as "She". We like to believe that this is because no two ships have the same temperament, that they have their difference of opinion, when answering to the helm, and are very difficult to handle. We refer to her "Waist" her "Ribs" her "Rear", and when we decorate the ship with coloured bunting and flags, "She is all dressed up".

THE ROYAL MARINES

One may very well ask, "what is a Royal Marine" and from different members of the Royal Navy you would get many and varied answers. A Bootneck, a Leatherneck, a Royal and some not very complimentary terms made after they had paraded on a freshly scrubbed deck, but all said with a deep sense of pride and not a little admiration for their record of achievements in all parts of the world.

Admiral Lord St Vincent said, "I never knew of an appeal made to them, for honour courage or loyalty in which they did not realise my highest expectations. If ever the hour of real danger should come to England, they will be found to be, the country's sheet anchor". Kipling described them thus, "a marine, you will find them all over the world, a'doing all kind of things, like landing himself with a Gatling gun, to talk to them heathen Kings."

The complements of H.M.Ships are comprised of a number of different Divisions. In the main they are, the Quarterdeckmen, the Focs'le men, the Topmen, the Communications and Signal branch, the Supply branch, the Torpedo branch and we would be very remiss if we failed to acknowledge the Engineering branch, "the Stokers". There are of course other small specialist branches without which the ship could not operate. And of course, there is the Royal Marine Detachment. All Royal Marine units are raised and paid by the Admiralty. They are ruled, not by the Army Regulations but by the Kings Rules and Admiralty Instructions and subject to Naval discipline.

They were first recruited into the Royal Navy in 1664 some three hundred and thirty three years ago. Almost two hundred years before Stokers came into being and approximately two hundred and fifty years before the Submarine Service and Fleet Air Arm came into being as newly formed arms of the Royal Navy.

A Royal Marine's uniform is of course very much different from that of his fellow shipmates, except in one respect. In common with the Officers, Chief Petty Officers, Petty Officers and all other ranks who wear jackets, their buttons are emblazoned with the "Fouled Anchor". A long time symbol of seafarers, the "Fouled Anchor" is the first much coveted symbol of authority awarded to the lower deck. It is the first big jump from "Ordinary Seaman" to "Leading Seaman". Herein after to be referred to as "Killick". So called after the type of anchor.

The Royal Marines, on Capital ships, usually man fifty per cent of the secondary armament, twenty five per cent of the main armament and almost fifty per cent of the ships air defence.

The Royal Marines Bandsmen, besides carrying out their duties as musicians are also responsible for manning the highly technical Transmitting Station in the bowels of the ship, without which, the ships massive fire power would be strictly limited.

It stands to reason therefore, that in all things Naval a Royal Marine is the equal of his "Comrades in Arms" and has earned the right to be called "Shipmate".

SPLICE THE MAINBRACE

"Splice the Mainbrace" was a presentation to
the ships companies of an extra tot of rum to
reward them for some very special act, or to
commemorate some very special occasion.
The order, to Splice the Mainbrace is not
given lightly. It was first ordered on the
Sovereign's birthday, but is very infrequently
given also for events of great national importance.

In olden times it was often given as reward
to the men who had the dangerous task of
splicing the mainbrace or mainmast in very
inclement weather at sea.

STARBOARD AND PORT

Originally the terms were Starboard and Larboard
and this sometimes led to confusion because of
the similarity. The Larboard side was always
alongside the jetty or dock wall and to facilitate
loading, a door was put into this side and called
a Port Hole. Eventually the whole side was then
change from Larboard to the Port Side. Thus Port
Side and Starboard Side came into being and so
remains to the present day.

CRUISERS

Cruiser, is, most people believe derived from the name "Crusal", a small lightly armed ship, used by the pirates in the Middle East. Used mainly for it's speed and not for fighting. It was one of the most efficient weapons in their pillaging and provided a quick getaway.

CROSSING THE LINE CELEBRATION

Long before the ceremony of "Crossing the International Date Line", there were similar ceremonials when going through "The Straits of Gibraltar" and when passing over the 39th parallel in the region of Lisbon, but it is not connected with the present day tributes to Neptune. The ceremony was quite simple and consisted of running between obstacles placed on the deck, whilst at the same time being drenched with water. Alternatively, the victims could choose to pay a fine.

SUNSET AROUND THE WORLD

Everyone is conversant with the ceremony of lowering the colours at Sunset on board every ship or establishment in every part of the world. In olden times, the Marine sentry always fired his rifle. This was to ensure that the old flintlock musket was loaded and primed for the night watches.

BOOTNECKS

"Bootnecks" is the nickname affectionately given by men of the Royal Navy, to the men of the Royal Marines serving on H.M.Ships. It is understood that the name was first derived by the use of a soft piece of smooth leather, similar to the tongue of a boot which was fastened behind the neck fastening on their rather hard collars. For the same reason, the United States Marines are at times referred to as "Leathernecks".

JACK TARS

Jack was a shortened name for jacket around the year 1600. At that time it was common practice for Sailors to cover their jacket and trousers in tar to make them waterproof and some wag christened the wearer "Jack Tar".

FORECASTLE MEN AND TOPMEN

The Forecastle, (Foc'sle) Men, were selected from the more experienced seamen and they worked at the front end of the ship, (The Bow), which was the furthest point from the Captain who was on the poop deck.

The neatest, fittest and most agile were the Topmen, who obviously worked on the rigging and at the mast heads.

MANNING SHIP'S SIDE

To man the ship's side was to show that your
ship's company was not manning the guns, It is
therefore to be assumed that your intentions
were friendly.

MAKING DEAD MEN CHEW

Was a reference to fraudulent pursers, who
supposedly sold tobacco to men who had died
in service. The term was used in the 1700's
for the pay and rations of men who had died,
deserted or had never even been in the service,
except as illegal names on the ships ledgers.
The purser would then pocket the profit.

FLOGGING AS A PUNISHMENT

The Cat-o-Nine tails was initiated by the French
and known as a Martinet. So named after a French
Colonel, the Marquis de Martinet, who was a great
believer in enforcing discipline.

GROG (NELSON'S BLOOD)

Grog, is watered down rum and was usually issued at the rate of two parts water to one part rum. One of the privileges of being a Petty Officer or Sergeant, Royal Marines was to draw your daily ration before it was watered down. After the issue was complete, My lords of Admiralty decreed that what was left must be poured down the scupper. This practice led to all sorts of "Official Cheating". The surplus was never wasted.

It is said that Admiral Vernon was the first to initiate the watering down of the raw spirit. As part of his dress he always wore a cloak of rough cloth called "Grogram". After his decree, he became known as "Old Grog", and the fleet composed a ditty which went as follows:-

A mighty tub of rum he drew
Almost to the brink,
Such drank the Burfords gallant crew
And such the Gods would drink.

The sacred "Robe" which Vernon wore
was drenched with all the same;
And hence it's virtues shall guard our shore
And "Grog" derived it's name.

I NAME THIS SHIP?

Late in the 17th century a silver cup was always used to drink the ship's health, after which, the cup was thrown overboard. This was said to be too expensive and a bottle was used thereafter, by the simple practice of smashing it on the bows. The ceremony was normally carried out by a royal personage, usually the Prince Regent. It was he who suggested that this part of the procedure should be carried out by one of the distinguished ladies present at the time. It is reported that one these ladies missed, and seriously injured a male spectator who sued the Admiralty for damages, after which, the bottle was secured by a lanyard, as it is to day.

WAISTERS

The term "waister" was often used to described a member of the ships company who was unable to work in the rigging, or carry out normal sea going duties because of his inexperience. The only duties that were available were those of menial nature in the waist of the ship and so earned him the term of reproach as a "Waister". And so it is today, in everyday life.

THE HEADS

The heads, or to be more precise these days, the ships company's toilets were always situated right in the prow of the ship. The prow was usually decorated with a bird of prey's beak or figurehead.
So to go to the toilet, you went to the head.

THE SHIP'S BELL

The bell is always on the quarter deck and is struck once for every half hour of a four hour watch. For example:- One bell, two bells, up to eight bells and then starts the next watch with one bell again on the first half hour. The "Dog" watches from 1600 to 2000 hrs are divided into two watches. 1600 hrs to 1800 hrs is the first Dog Watch and 1800 hrs to 2000 hrs is the second Dog Watch. After which, the four hour watches start again.

An old explanation as to why they are referred to as the "Dog Watches", is that an Admiral once spoke of them as the watches that were "Cur Tailed".

WHY SPEED IS MEASURED IN KNOTS

To define the speed in knots, a number of equally spaced knots were tied along a length of rope which trailed behind the ship, in conjunction with a sand glass. The number of knots which ran out in a marked measure in the sand glass was logged as speed of the ship.

THE QUARTER DECK (THE HOLY OF HOLIES)

The rear quarter of the Upper Deck, to the modern day sailor is the Quarter Deck, it is sacrosanct and is to be avoided unless you are on official business. It is normally the officers "Walkabout", and where defaulters are taken before The Officer of the Watch for minor offences. It is usually kept in a spotless condition by constant scrubbing by the Quarterdeck men, using the abrasive blocks known as "Holy Stones".

THE MESS DECK

From the Spanish "Mesa" meaning table, or from the Latin "Mensa", i.e. Table deck, or where the men live.

HOLY STONES

Holy stones are so called because they have to be used in the kneeling position and is one of the hardest duties carried out when cleaning ship. An ancient ditty written by Naval authors in the past goes as follows:-

Eight bells were struck, poor Jack awoke
Before the dawn of day had broke
And mustered round the Capstan he
Picked up "The Stone" and bent his knee.
He bent his knee, but not in prayer
He was cursing the man who sent him there.

SHOW A LEG

"Show a Leg" dates back to the days when women were allowed to "Lie In", after the morning call when the men went to work. To prove that it really was a women in the hammock they had to hang one of their legs over the side. Even in those days, there was obviously a difference.

TELL IT TO THE MARINES

Tell it to the Marines is a saying used by many of us in every day use, without really knowing why. Pepys, was relating to Charles II that the Captain of HMS Defiance had stated in conversation that he had actually seen fish flying above the level of the sea. The Royal Courtiers refused to believe such an absurd statement, until Sir William Kellegrew, an officer of the Maritime Regiment of Foot, the forerunners of the Royal Marines, said that he himself had seen this on many occasions. Whereupon, the King, turned to Pepys and said, "From the very nature of their calling, no class of our subjects has so wide a knowledge of the seas than our loyal Officers and men of the Maritime Regiments. Henceforward, err we cast doubt on a tale that lacks likelihood, we will first tell it to the Marines".

HARRY FREEMAN'S

"Harry Freeman's" in the services, usually meant getting something for nothing. The term dates back to the time when Harry Freeman was a warehouseman in Tooley Street, near to Tower Bridge, London. It was always his practice to give free beer to the Porters who carried for him.

THE LADY OF THE GUNROOM

The Gunner was usually in charge of the Gunroom and in his list of instructions was the entry that, a responsible member of his crew was to stand watch every night with a candle in a lantern and at the same time to keep the Gunroom clean. This watchman was known as the "Lady of the Gunroom" and the store below was known as "The Lady's Hole".

MARINES BARRACKS

The Marines living quarters or Messdeck as it was more commonly called, was always situated between the Officers and the remainder of the ships company, as were all the ammunition and the small arms racks. This was by the orders of Admiral Lord St Vincent who was a great admirer of the Maritime Regiment. It was he who said, "I never knew an appeal made to them for Honour, Courage or Loyalty, In which they did not realise my greatest expectations, if ever the hour of real danger should come to England, they will be proved the country's sheet anchor."

THE SHEET ANCHOR

The "Sheet Anchor" was an especially heavy and strong anchor, thrown over the stern of the ship in extremes of weather or when the ship was in any sort of danger, i.e. rocks etc. It was hoped that this would have a steadying effect on the ship and so neutralise the danger.

OFFICERS OF THE ROYAL NAVY

Early in the beginning of the eighteenth century the Royal Navy had only three officers of the rank of Admiral. The three separate fleets referred to as the Red Squadron, the Blue Squadron and the White Squadron were commanded by a senior officer of Admiral rank. Of these three units the Admiral commanding the Red Squadron was the one chosen to be in charge of all three Squadrons and was referred to thereafter as the Admiral of the Fleet.

For some unknown reason the title of Admiral was originated from Arabic source. The translation came from the Arabic rank of Emir El Bahr, which in the parlance of the day, roughly meant "Lord of the Sea". It was many years later, around the middle of the sixteenth century that the rank of Vice Admiral was initiated and the rank of Rear Admiral was brought into being about the end of the same century.

It was in the middle of the 1860's, the different colours for the three fleets were to be abolished and the whole of the Royal Navy were instructed to fly the White Ensign. It should be mentioned at this time that there was in existence a fourth fleet with the title of the Yellow Fleet a purely imaginary fleet created by Admiral Anson and presumed to be a shore billet for newly promoted Admirals.

Below the rank of Admiral comes the rank of Commodore, a temporary rank, which previously had been the rank held by the senior rank of the merchant fleet.

CAPTAIN

Captains were first appointed about the beginning of the thirteenth century and they were not originally Naval Officers, their initial duties were to command the soldiers taking passage. It became apparent that they would have to have a working knowledge of the ships routine and as a consequence were accepted as ships officers.

COMMANDER

The rank of Commander in charge of small ships created some difficulty between them and the senior officers of some of the larger ships in the Royal Navy. They were often referred to as "Masters", "Sub Captains", etc. After the heavy recruitment during the Napoleonic Wars, surplus Commanders on the Navy lists were appointed to serve on Battleships as secondary Captains or No 2 Captains and the rank was thus established.

LIEUTENANT COMMANDER

Was established at the beginning of the first world war in 1914, although in actual fact the extra half ring had been worn by Lieutenants who had served eight years or more since the middle of the 1870's.

LIEUTENANT

There have been Lieutenants in the Royal Navy since the latter end of the sixteenth Century and only one was appointed to each command and was solely to train them as future Captains.

SUB LIEUTENANTS

Was a rank brought into being to reward Midshipmen who had passed their examinations for Lieutenant, but who had to wait for a vacancy on the Navy List. It was instituted by Admiral Lord St Vincent, famous for his statement, that, "If ever the hour of danger should come to England, the Royal Marines would prove to be the country's sheet anchor".

MIDSHIPMEN

Were so called after they had served seven years before the mast and were able to navigate the ship. They were then and still are to this day referred to as "Snotties", a title bestowed upon them because of their habit of wiping their noses on the cuff of their jacket. In an attempted to prevent this, when the decorative buttons were removed from the Officers uniforms, the three buttons on the sleeves of the Midshipmens jackets were retained.

OTHER RANKS AND TITLES

There were of course many other ranks and titles, all of them relating to the duties of the person concerned. There were the Surgeons, the Paymasters, the Chaplains, Inspectors of Machinery and Gunners.

IN THE BEGINNING

The "Thirties" were years of poverty
Starvation and existing in slums,
The despised and hated "Means Test"
And an attitude of taking what comes.

The tenements reared their ugly heads
Families lived in despair,
The "Rachman" types made their fortune
And it seemed that no one could care.

The North West had it's quota of hellspots
Employment could not be lower,
And pushed together in crowded rooms
Morality had flown out of the door.

It was a breeding place for Incest
Prostitution, thieving and rape,
Where the policemen went about in pairs
Armed with the deadly "Cape".

The Cape was fastened with lions heads
Large and joined with a chain,
And quite often used as weapons
Inflicting great hurt and pain.

But, we respected our police of yesteryear
They had sympathy for our sort,
And receiving a clip from the deadly Cape
Was much better than going to court.

They were not just "Tools of Government"
They were Advisor, Father or Friend,
And no one could ever envisage
That the system was soon to end.

For the Cape was now changed for the Book of Rules
To be enforced, up to the hilt,
No longer was there an in between
On which the friendships had been built.

The Ghettos formed in Cheetham Hill
Where the Jews collected in droves,
The fent and rag shops infested with lice
Were the future treasure troves.

From these very humble beginnings
Where they sweated for a miserable pay,
The Cohens, The Marks and The Jacobs
Became "The Rag Trade" of today.

To escape from an environment at it's lowest ebb
Was the desire of most in their teens,
Most chose the Army or the Navy
My choice was the Royal Marines.

I passed my test of English and Maths
Collected my "Shilling" and swore,
An oath of allegiance to my King
For twelve long years or more.

An oath I think I have faithfully kept
For all over the world I have been,
Involved in a war for six long years
So proud to be called "A Marine".

It all started off as a rookie
A recruit in the Depot, at Deal,
Where I sweated and tore my heart out
Determined to make my dream real.

For weeks and months I pounded the square
My rifle became part of my arm,
I hated the guts of my instructor
Who was not renowned for his charm.

In the field it was no different
The rivers deep and the mountains high,
The pools of mud were placed just right
Right in the place, I was told to lie.

But sometime the torture had to end
They hadn't spared the rod,
We finished as perfect as perfect could be
The "Ultimate", finished, "King's Squad".

The blood, the sweat, the pain and tears
Were not quite over yet,
For now it was the turn of "The Gunnery School"
To make sure that we didn't forget.

Discipline and discipline, and yet even more
For gunnery was a serious drill,
Mens lives depended upon your speed
A speed matched only by skill.

Four inch, six inch and eight inch guns
And the massive fifteen inch,
I became an expert in all of these
To me they were all a cinch.

It became of course an obvious fact
That while others fought on land,
I would be posted to fight at sea
Just the way I had planned.

For it was exciting to sit in your metal seat
With the "Churn Lever" in your hand,
And the noise of loading the fifteen inch
Would drown out the Royal Marine Band.

The crashing of steel, the hissing of air
I felt proud of all I saw,
My gun crew were perfect, in all that they did
We were finished, we were ready for war.

THE SPANISH CIVIL WAR 1936

Spain was in a turmoil
In the midst of a civil war,
As Brother slaughtered Brother
And nobody knew what for.

It was a training ground for "The Axis"
As the bombers roared overhead,
Good practice for Herr Goering
His masters were looking ahead.

Outside the three mile limit
In the Bay they call "Biscay",
The "Gun Runners", stood off and waited
For the first grey light of day.

If the Cervantes and the Cervera
Were no where to be seen,
It was full speed ahead for Santandar
Bilbao, or some where between.

They unloaded their guns and weapons of death
Then drew their pay and left,
No thoughts of the thousands lying dead
Or the hundreds of children bereft.

It happened one day, one was caught in the act
The Spanish Cruisers had him to rights,
"Spud Jones", the notorious "Runner of Guns"
Was lined up quite plain in their sights.

But with an escort of "B" Class Destroyers
The Resolution, hove into view,
And warned the Spanish Cruisers
Not to carry it through.

With the Bulldog and the Brazen
One , each side of the Tramp,
The Reso' sent out a signal
Flashing on an Aldis Lamp.

"We are here to protect our nationals
If to sink them is your desire,
Then please do not hit my Destroyers
Or I shall certainly open fire."

With his fifteen inch trained outboard
There's no doubt he would have fired,
So the Spaniards in their wisdom
Signalled "Adios Senor" and retired.

Dorling recalled his Destroyers
And went upon his way,
"Spud Jones" even signalled "Thank you"
And lived for another day.

DUNKIRK

The B.E.F. were stranded
On the sands of "La Belle France",
The German hordes surrounded them
They didn't stand a chance.

For France had given up the ghost
And too quickly, laid down their guns,
The Dutch and the Belgians had followed suit
Over run by the speeding Huns.

In the dunes and on the beaches
Hungry, tired and suffering with thirst,
Tens of thousands of British troops
Could only sit and fear the worst.

But further West near Plymouth Hoe
A muffled beat echoed over the sand,
"Drakes Drums", had started beating
And the beat floated over the land.

The muffled beat of the ancient drum
As it did in the days of yore,
Rolled along the English coast
And echoed on the English shore.

The ghostly beat, rolled up the coves
The inlets, rivers and streams,
And Mariners, all over the land
Awoke from their slumbers and dreams.

From the waterways inlets and rivers
Came the fishing boats steamers and yachts,
And those that only yesterday
Were gathering their lobster pots.

Young men, just earning their laurels
Old sailors, Well past their prime,
Pushed their old craft to their limits
Determined to be next in the line.

They struggled against the Foreland tides
And some were even taken in tow,
Their engines were weak, but their hearts were strong
As one man they intended to go.

As the British armada came into view
The Army rushed into the sea,
They helped each other to the nearest boats
Crying "Thank God" and "Wait for me".

Those "Weekend sailors", had pulled it off
The expeditionary force had been saved,
"The British Army lives to fight again"
The next days headlines raved.

And as the old weary sailors, took their tired crews home
Their ears ringing with "Thanks for the ride",
Raleigh, Collingwood, Nelson and Drake with his "Drum"
Looked down on a Nation's pride.

THE WAY TO THE STARS

From the South of the South Atlantic
To the North of the Northern Pole,
They guarded the oceans convoys
For such was the warships role.

There were many who died in those ice cold seas
And many still carry the scar,
But those that remain can walk erect
For they wear "The Atlantic Star".

From Sidi Barrani to Tripoli
Was one hell of a walk to take,
Benghazi, Torbruk and El Alemain
Were not just "Pieces of Cake".

The flies, the heat, the shelling
The fighting that started each dawn,
Brings back the beat to many a heart
On which "The Africa Star" is worn.

Then it's onwards up from Leghorn
And all the way to Rome,
They drove the Panzers Northwards
It was another step nearer home.

Admittedly the price was high
As thousands crossed "The Bar",
And for giving their life for their country
They now wear "The Italy Star".

29

From England they sailed in their thousands
The Channel was covered with ships,
The coast of France was an armoured fort
And these were no pleasure trips.

They swept on and ever onwards
The Empire, the "Old" and the "New",
All the way to Berlin and back
And the rows of graves just grew.

To save the world from destruction
The Armies came from afar,
They paid with their lives for our freedom
And "The France and Germany Star".

So now we go to India
Rangoon and the Burma Trail,
The Irriwaddy and the Arakan
Only tweaking the Japanese tail.

It took the Fourteenth Army
And "The Chindits" who travelled so far,
To tie a knot in the Nipponese tail
And come home with "The Burma Star".

There were those that went ever Eastwards
Towards "The Land of the Rising Sun",
Supporting the Yanks and the Anzacs
Who now had the Nips on the run.

The Nips turned those beautiful islands
Into graves for those who would say,
"When you go home please tell them,
For their tomorrow's we gave our today".

It was sad as we turned for our homeland
We had fought and travelled so far,
We had cried and bled, and buried our dead
And for what, "The Pacific Star".

We came home to a Country so grateful
Our Leaders had promised the Earth,
And fifty years on we're still struggling
And fighting for what we are worth.

The "Youth", that performed those deeds long ago
Are the "Pensioners" of today
"Ah!, but you never had it so good"
We now here the Leaders say.

Meanwhile the standards of our former foes
Get better year after year,
It is we "The Victors" who are losing the fight
And it's getting worse I fear.

So, it's up to you all to remember
For our numbers are getting less,
And we wouldn't like it to happen again
And it could very well. God Bless.

A TRIBUTE TO "THE FEW"

We honour our younger warriors
Creating slipstreams in the sky,
The deeds of valour performed on the ground
Are repeated way up on high.

The "Erks" from Grammar and Public schools
The hairs on their faces quite new,
Changed overnight from boys to men
And came to be known as "The Few".

They formed a barrier in the sky
Of Hurricanes and Spit's,
They faced great odds and gave their all
To throw back the promised Blitz.

They were not just Brit's who perished
The Poles and Yanks were there,
Canadians, Free French and Aussies
And New Zealanders with their flair.

South Africans, Indians, who else can we say
Yes the Dutch and Belgians as well,
And volunteers from all over the world
Helped the lists of dead to swell.

Their names are written in vapour
The trails still there in the sky,
And they wear their "Air Crew Stars" with pride
As the cry "Tally Ho" whispers by.

THE PRISON SHIP, ALTMARK

The German "U" Boats prowled the seas
Looking for easy prey,
Merchantmen, alone, unarmed
Were sunk, day after day.

Sometimes the crew were left to die
Some "Lucky Ones" plucked from the sea,
To be prisoners on the Altmark
The "Hellship" of the sea.

For Hitler had sworn to parade them
To the citizens of Berlin,
To march them through the streets in chains
He thought it would help him win.

But I don't think he quite knew our navy
And the deep rooted pride in it's sons,
For with every ship on the lookout
They restricted the Altmark's runs.

Then, somewhere in the cold North Sea
This Hellship came to light,
And preferred the safety of a neutral port
To facing the Navy's might.

She fled the length of Josing Fjord
The prisoners still locked in her hold,
While out at sea, the Cossack
Awaiting a plan to unfold.

With direct orders from Churchill
"That this Hellship shall not reach Berlin,"
The Cossack breached the laws of a neutral state
And as night fell, steamed right in.

In the dark, she slid alongside
As they did in days of old,
And crying out "The Navy's Here"
Ripped the covers off the Focs'le hold.

Three hundred and three gaunt faces looked up
There were tears on the faces of some,
"It took you a bloody long time" said one
"But we knew all a long you would come."

THE SECOND BATTLE OF NARVIK – 13th APRIL 1940

To the North of the Arctic Circle
"Our Lords" had said "You Must Go,
Our Destroyers have taken a hiding
And you must destroy the foe".

A large force of German Destroyers
Patrolling the Cold Arctic Sea,
Had attacked some Home Fleet Destroyers
Commanded by Warburton Lee.

They had caused real havoc off Narvik
Then sought cover deep in their hides,
To them there was no safer harbour
Protected so well on all sides.

Shore Batteries and shore based Torpedoes
And no doubt a minefield or two,
But the British forces bent on revenge
Knew what they had to do.

The veteran Battle ship Warspite
And Destroyers of the sleek Tribal Class,
Were soon to put the fear of God
In the hearts of the top German Brass.

They swept fast like "The Light Brigade" of old
Through the Fjords of white virgin snow,
The destroyers fired with all that they had
Then, the Warspites turrets let go.

They turned that peaceful white Fjord
Into "Dante's Inferno" no less.
Ship after ship settled down on her keel
Quite soon they were all in distress.

35

Ten ships in all the enemy lost
Revenge had been short and sweet,
Then the Warspite and her Destroyers
Retired, to rejoin the Fleet.

At full speed they hit open water
Soon bombers would be well on their track,
They had beaten the best that the enemy had
But now was the time to get back.

We made it safely to our Northern base
To the locals, we had been out on a run,
But the Fleet, in the know, cheered loud as we passed
And all, flew the signal, "Well Done".

MURDER AT SEA

A ship steamed on in the darkness
Leaving a phosphorous trail,
Her bow cut deep into a seething sea
White froth smashing over her rail.

The hum of her powerful turbines
The throbbing of each giant screw,
Appeared to implant a soothing effect
In the brains of her sleeping crew.

But the hum and the throbbing that soothed below
Was wasted way up on high,
For while the watch on the bridge paced up and down
Tired eyes searched a stygian sky.

But out there it seemed was a blind spot
For a small florescent trail,
Was travelling fast on a parallel course
At a distance that could not fail.

"Fire two and four" the order came
"And for good luck, fire number five,
Then it's home to Bremerhaven
Thanking GOD that we're still alive".

As he turned for home and his Iron Cross
Three torpedoes sped on their way,
The three of them struck, one fore, one aft
And one midships where sleeping men lay.

In moments the massacre was over
Flames and scalding steam filled the air,
The crew that were able, chose the cold of the sea
And over all was an air of despair.

Down first, went the bow and then followed the stern
The raging fires suppressed by the sea,
The few that survived clung together and sang
"Oh hear us as we cry to thee".

But the wet and the cold of that fateful night
Took it's toll of the ship and it's men,
And with the first light of dawn, there was nothing to see
And all was peaceful again.

CONVOYS

The Convoy steamed slowly Northwards
And soon would be turning East,
And hiding in the depths below
Slid a sleek ferocious beast.

The "U" Boats were silent and deadly
They prowled the seas in packs,
Looking for Tramps and Tankers
Betrayed by the smoke from their stacks.

The speed of the Convoy, is the slowest ship
If one falters, when doing her best,
Then she is left to fend for herself
So as not to endanger the rest.

As the Convoy steamed on it's zig zag course
A Tramp was left far astern,
A long way from where she was going
But too far out to return.

In the periscope of the leading Sub'
The Tramp has come into view,
A perfect strike for the surface gun
And practice for the crew.

The leading Sub', now leaves the pack
And lines up for the kill,
Nothing to fear from the stricken Tramp
Just a routine drill.

The range is perfect, the target is hit
How can one miss, almost touching the hull,
Shell after shell, burst on her decks
The sea boats are swamped because they're too full.

Somewhere a machine gun chatters
Fingers gripping the Sub', let go,
Then suddenly the Tramp rears up
Only the barnacles show.

Boats and floats are pulling away
To get clear of the suction field,
One more lurch, and down she goes
Her fate now finally sealed.

The Sub's Commander, clears the bridge
"Flood one and two fore", he cried,
Down went the Sub' to periscope depth
No regrets for those who had died.

Aboard the Tramp as she slid down to the deep
A Morse key kept tapping away,
A W/T had stayed at his post
And sent out his last "May Day".

Just over the horizon, a sleek grey shape
From the North Atlantic Fleet,
Steamed one of the "Working Greyhounds"
Out on a Submarine beat.

The Commander had just read a signal
"Full speed ahead" he cried,
"All hands to action stations"
And the "Greyhound" broke into her stride.

Soon reaching the scene of the slaughter
With boats lowered over the side,
She slowed and picked up survivors
As well as those that had died.

And then she went a'hunting
Increasing the circle each round,
Until "The Asdic" finally pinged
The quarry, a Sub', had been found.

The control then worked out a pattern
The depth charges hurled into the air,
Then dropped in a diamond formation
To trap the beast in his lair.

It was during the fourth or fifth salvo
That the white frothy spume turned black,
A Submarine's hull reared out of the sea
Rolled over, and then slid back.

The Tramp's survivors stood up and cheered
But most stood silent head bowed,
For sending a ship with her crew to the depths
Was not something of which to be proud.

You can only think of the deeds she has done
Performed in the Fuhrer's name,
And say "They have only been paid the wages of sin"
It's all in the luck of the game.

DAWN ACTION STATIONS

We cruised along at our cruising speed
Three quarters of the crew sound asleep,
The other quarter stood around their guns
They had a watch to keep.

The time was o'four fifty
The sky was inky black,
The exhausted crews of the middle watch
Had just about hit the sack.

The operators in the Radar room
Were watching the screen for blips,
But the only blips at that moment
Were those of friendly ships.

For we were in powerful company
Cruisers on the quarters and beam,
And far out on the screen, the Destroyers
Quite a formidable team.

The lookouts searched the surface
For a continuous florescent line,
Caused by a speeding periscope
Quite a give-away sign.

The Duty Officer patrolling the bridge
Looked at his watch and said,
"I'll call the Captain, you call the hands"
Then continued his stately tread.

The quartermaster opened the tannoy
Cleared his throat and said,
"All hands to action stations"
In a voice that would waken the dead.

Hammocks were swiftly vacated
And then removed with all speed,
Then off to your General Quarters
Just as the tannoy decreed.

There's a place for each man in the pattern
As every man knows to his pain,
Each and everyone is important
There's no weak links in this chain.

The Layers and Trainers followed their dials
Traversing their guns through the arks,
Ammunition provided and ready to load
We were not just closed up for larks.

Dawn Action Stations was a serious drill
Far as darkness turned to light,
The horizon could be broken by enemy ships
Like us, all ready to fight.

After an hour, when the sky was bright
And the lookouts reported "All Clear",
The order came for all to stand down
For today, there was nothing to fear.

The cooks returned to their galley
No time to stand and yawn,
For a thousand plus souls were hungry
And once again, a new day had been born.

THE MALTA RUN

The turret was still and silent
The crew were at their dials,
The air inside was stale and dead
As their thoughts travelled over the miles.

It had been many a month since leaving our shore
Months that were etched on each face,
A subtle smile would sometimes break through
A memory of that last embrace.

Was it a Mother, Father, or newly wed Wife
A Sweetheart, a Daughter, or Son,
Or just a memory of that last night out
Before joining "The Malta Run".

Africa lay well off to the South
Italy was well out of sight,
And not far off in the morning mist
Pantellaria, would soon be in sight.

A fortress of Axis bombers
Ready to fly into the Sun,
Had heard from their spies in Gibraltar
That a Convoy, was "Making the Run".

You could almost hear the engines roar
As they taxied, then took to the sky,
Flight after flight of enemy planes
Determined that Malta should die.

The Fleet had ringed the Tankers
The orders had passed to the guns,
To throw up an umbrella of shells
But nothing could put off the Huns.

They came from every direction
The best that Goering could send,
The Tankers had no chance at all
In the main they followed the trend.

One after one, they floundered on fire
Palls of smoke spiralled into the sky,
The dead and the dying were floating in oil
For the most it were better to die.

But as always the agony had to end
We were approaching our Eastern Fleet,
The Carrier they had, had sent up her planes
The attackers were now in retreat.

The survivors limped into Malta
Their "Red Dusters" torn, but unfurled,
They had paid the price for delivering the goods
But the cost was out of this World.

We, in our turrets, still watched our dials
But our thoughts now started to roam,
They were now with those who had perished that day
And who would never again sail home.

So let us hope as the years pass by
And the War is either lost or won,
That we remember with pride, the men who had died
Whilst making "The Malta Run".

THE AFRICAN CAMPAIGN

The British and Commonwealth troops held fast
To a dirty North African town,
Backwards and forwards, they won, then lost,
No wonder their spirits were down.

Stores were low, the food was poor
And they faced a formidable foe,
For "The Desert Fox" was a name to fear
And they had a long way to go.

Flanking the road to Tripoli
The tank parks held the pass,
For Rommel's strength was his Tiger Tanks
And as Tanks go, they were class.

But, silently, just out of sight
The Navy brought out it's big guns,
And as dawn streaked the sky, they opened fire
And poured "Broadsides" into the Huns.

The Tank Parks erupted in geysers of sand
The "Tigers" for once outclassed,
They rose in the air like "Dinky Toys"
Destroyed by a power unsurpassed.

For the powers that be in London
Had seen the light at last,
They ordered "The Eighth" in Africa
To sit tight, regroup and hold fast.

Around the Cape and through the Med'
On ships both large and small,
Came the Planes, the Tanks and the Field Guns
There seemed no end to it all.

They also sent Montgomery
Small in stature, it's true,
But he commanded the respect of all of his men
Yes, and even the enemy too.

He outgunned and outfought Rommel
And started to force him back,
Starting the push at El Alemain
And Rommel started to crack.

Slowly Montgomery countered and thrust
His expertise was supreme,
His troops and equipment, now proved to be best
And so ended "The Africa Corps dream".

Tripoli was the end of the line
Sad to say, many graves lined the route,
But the Commonwealth troops marched tall and proud
As Monty, took the salute.

CALABRIA

It was hot closed up in the Gunhouse
And we were stripped to the waist,
And to dress up in "Anti Flash" gear
Wasn't quite up to our taste.

The turret wall was ten inches thick
The air inside, hot and dead,
We stood and shuffled in a yard of space
On feet that felt like lead.

The young Lieutenant sat on his high seat
Perspiring, while the rest of us sweat,
As usual relying on his N.C.O's,
While he worked out his mess bill debt.

Then, disturbing the calm of the Gunhouse
The dials began to tick round,
The Communicator adjusted his phones
To hear what the Director had found.

A blip on the far horizon
Gave warning of an enemy ship,
We sent up the Swordfish for spotting
Set the range and made allowance for "Dip".

We had loaded with Armour Piercing
A full charge of Cordite as well,
And we stood there awaiting the recoil
That would shortly follow the bell.

The Trainer moved slowly his pointers
The Layer went to maximum range,
For any other ship to engage like this
Would indeed have seemed quite strange.

But the Warspite was a gunnery ship
A ship that had never yet quit,
And we opened fire at more than fifteen miles
And the very first Salvo hit.

The enemy Battleship, turned and ran
It was a complete rout,
And although severely damaged
Her speed was never in doubt.

We were now so near to the enemy coast
We were well in the bombers path,
So we turned and made our way to base
To avoid retaliatory wrath.

Alexandria wasn't such a pleasant place
But it was heaven on earth to me,
To sit with memories of a job well done
In a bar, with a view of the sea.

TARANTO

The Italians were superior in numbers
Their Battleships modern and fast,
But their hearts were not in the conflict
And in experience were well outclassed.

Most days they stayed safely in harbour
Only occasionally going out on a foray,
And only then, when the British Fleet
Was hundreds of miles away.

The answer then, seemed so simple
To hit them where it hurt,
To attack them in their "Hidey Hole"
And rub El Duce's nose in the dirt.

So the Fleet, reduced to one Carrier
Left Alex' on a normal sweep West,
And, for the always present observers
Our intentions were kept close to our chest.

The Illustrious was our floating "Drome"
Her strike planes not exactly the best,
But the men who flew those Swordfish
Were a cut above the rest.

The evening sun had now submerged
The time was eight thirty p.m.,
When the thundering roar of twenty one planes
Was heard by the listening men.

South East of Taranto, they took to the sky
Ken Williamson leading his flight,
Norman (Blood) Scarlett, showed him the way
As they travelled in the evening light.

The first wave of twelve went into a dive
The "Littorio" in their sights down below,
Their torpedoes released for a perfect strike
Seemed to travel, ever so slow.

Slow they might seem, or so it appeared
But down below it was clear,
That the "Littorio" and the "Conte di Cavour"
At that moment, knew the meaning of fear.

The second strike down, three Battleships hit
Fire and thick smoke filled the air,
But by now, getting out was a difficult job
For Flak bursts were everywhere.

Ken Williamson turned his brood homewards
The attack had been a success,
But sad to say, as he checked his brood
He now counted two chicks less.

It is never a clear cut victory
When four brave men are lost,
But when you set out to finish a job
You can never count the cost.

Mussolini had laid claim to the "Italian Lake"
But his word was never his bond,
For after that night at Taranto
"His Lake" became "Cunningham's Pond".

MATAPAN 1941

Or should we say "Master Plan". For months the Italian Navy had avoided a direct confrontation with the British Fleet, commanded by Admiral Andrew Cunningham, so it was decided to give them a little encouragement. The British Fleet were in harbour and normal recreational leave ashore was being enjoyed by the various ships companies.

Admiral Cunningham and his staff had made a great show of going ashore himself, complete with the necessary golfing equipment for a pleasant afternoon's relaxation. But, within minutes of landing, he made a detour and returned to his flagship. Meanwhile the various ships companies were instructed by various means to return to their ships.

Below decks, preparations had been put in hand for a speedy exit from the harbour. Without making smoke, steam had been raised for maximum knots, anchors had been taken in and ships remained moored to their buoys, ready for a quick slip of the cables. All boats had been left inboard and side ladders and booms were rigged ready for hoisting as soon as the order to get under way was given.

We must assume that the exercise was a complete success, the Italian Fleet, acting on information that the Royal Navy was safely in harbour, had put themselves in a position, where it was impossible for them to reach the safety of their base without having a direct confrontation with Cunningham's force.

The entire plan went without a hitch, the British force were waiting as the unsuspecting Italian ships made their way back to base.

The result, as we now know, was a victory for the Royal Navy in their first major night action and was to be recognised in Naval History as "The Battle of Cape Matapan".

THE BATTLE OF MATAPAN

Alexandria was way astern
Our bow was pointed West,
The enemy fleet had put to sea
And soon would face the test.

Two Cruisers teased them Southwards
Such a tempting bait,
Ere dawn had broken in the East
One side would know their fate.

In the dark we lay and waited
All our guns trained on the beam,
Shells and cordite, fully loaded
Breeches closed, a Gunners dream.

Three ships they came a'sailing
The Pola, Zara, Fiume,
In line ahead with guns secured
They were sailing to their doom.

Ahead of them in the darkness
Having laid the bait,
The Warspite, Valiant and Barham
Patiently lay in wait.

The escort ships on either beam
With searchlight, torpedo and gun,
Awaited the Flagship's signal
In case they decided to run.

For this was a game of cat and mouse
The mouse was approaching his hole,
And lying in wait was the craftiest cat
That ever played the role.

The Radar bleeped it's signal
The enemy is on the screen,
Still we lay and waited
Unheard, as yet unseen.

Then at the given signal
Blazing Starshells dropped astern,
Three enemy ships in silhouette
Sitting ducks just ready to turn.

The Searchlights hit them fair and square
The guns crews took their time,
The crossed wires on their gunsights
Lined up on the plimsol line.

The intercepting contacts made
The "Ting Ting" of the bell,
The Director Layer had made his play
And opened the gates of Hell.

The turrets spewed their lethal load
The sky erupted in light,
The flame and heat from exploding shells
Was not a pretty sight.

Like Roman Candles their magazines blazed
It was carnage form stem to stern,
As we turned and made our way to base
Leaving them there to burn.

The smaller ships looked for survivors
And plucked them from the sea,
For sailors are sailors all over the World
Saying, "Thou shalt not die by me".

There was no joy in victory
As there is no joy in death,
And safely in our naval base
We prayed beneath our breath.

The battle had been quick and fierce
Now beneath the waves they lie,
And said in the hearts of every man
"But for the Grace of God go I".

Today is a day of victory
Or so the headlines ran,
But to them and to us, it was just a word
And that word was "Matapan".

THE CATASTROPHE THAT WAS CRETE

"Hold that Island", My Lords had said
"Hold it for what" we cried,
"Never mind for what, just hold it" they said
And holding it, many of us died.

For it had no real significance
It was neither here nor there,
It had no rich ores or priceless crops
But for grapes, it was almost bare.

As a base it was less than useless
In fact Sude Bay was a trap,
In no way could ships use their radar
A most dangerous spot on the map.

But hold it we did for seven long months
From the month of November to May,
And then, when we were ordered to leave
That's when we had to pay.

Three Battleships and one Carrier damaged
Six Cruisers wrecked and three lost,
Six Destroyers sunk, seven of no further use
And that wasn't the end of the cost.

With the Carrier damaged and of no further use
With no Aircraft support for the Fleet,
One thousand eight hundred Sailors had died
We had to admit defeat.

Yes, we had our moments of valour
The fighting had not been one way,
There were names that would live on in History
As of yore on Trafalgar Day.

So if there's to be another mistake
Like the one that happened that May,
Then send out the Politicians
At least to earn some of their pay.

For it's easy to sit in comfort at home
Doing deals with a nod and a wink,
But to go out and die, for a stupid mistake
Would at least make them sit back and think.

For if Politicians had to stand up and fight
Instead of dreaming up laws,
Then there would be peace all over the World
And an end to all stupid Wars.

The lives that were lost for that barren Isle
Were lives that were wasted in vain,
"My Lords", might stand and bare their heads
But it's the people that bear the pain.

THE ROYAL MARINES SIX INCH BATTERY

May the 22nd., Nineteen Forty One
And the forenoon watch was mine,
The Bugler had sounded the rum call
At that moment all things were fine.

A short time more and my watch would be done
I was famished and ready for lunch,
When my opposite number relieved me
Then it was, came the crunch.

At just after one, he took my place
And took command of my crew,
With a grateful wave, I went below
He was now in charge of S.2.

But up on top deck, things had really got hot
"Alarm, Aircraft Red" was the cry,
Three Stuka's came streaking out of the sun
The Dive Bombers were having a try.

There was no safe way for the helm to go
They were spread across the width of our beam,
One of them hit, I know not which
It tore through the steel with a scream.

Down past the Starboard Pom Pom deck
Smashing through the four inch twin,
Then down to the Starboard six inch guns
There was no describing the din.

I stood on the Messdeck still vibrating with shock
The armoured doors buckling with heat,
Then I made my way back, from whence I had come
Not knowing what sight I would meet.

The side of the ship had lifted right up
Four gun barrels were swinging inside,
The rest of the Battery, was carnage indeed
A furnace where brave men had died.

A gold braided Commander was down on his knees
Praying, or so I thought then,
But coolly and calmly, he was injecting morphine
Into what was left of his men.

A lot of my shipmates perished that day
Sailors as well as Marines,
They were the best that the Forces had had
And many were just in their teens.

That night we stood guard on our Messdeck
The shrouded bodies in rows,
We said prayers for them and their loved ones
With a deep burning hate for our foes.

The next day was a day of remembrance
Even Sailors now learned how to weep,
We sang "Oh hear us as we cry to thee"
As each body sank to the deep.

I stood and watched in silence
It was hard not to remember and cry,
I mumbled over those well known words
"But for the Grace of God go I".

CRETE: - ROLL OF HONOUR

MAY 1941

SUNK:
H.M.S. Southampton
H.M.S. Calcutta
H.M.S. York
H.M.S. Juno
H.M.S. Greyhound
H.M.S. Gloucester
H.M.S. Fiji
H.M.S. Kelly
H.M.S. Kashmir
H.M.S. Hereward
H.M.S. Imperial

DAMAGED:
H.M.S. Warspite
H.M.S. Valiant
H.M.S. Formidable
H.M.S. Barham
H.M.S. Dido
H.M.S. Orion
H.M.S. Perth
H.M.S. Naiad
H.M.S. Ajax
H.M.S. Illustrious

KILLED IN ACTION

1,828

WOUNDED IN ACTION

183

REPAIRS AFTER CRETE 1941-1942

Crete was some days behind us
The damage we knew was severe,
It will take a long time to repair us
But we shall be back never fear.

As stated before, we had looked after our dead
Respectfully buried at sea,
The wounded and burned we had sent ashore
Now, what will the next move be.

So secret were the orders
We left in the dead of night,
Then silently sped through the Suez
To be clear by morning light.

We were travelling "Incognito"
Keeping well away from land,
We could only guess by the rising sun
The course that the Staff had planned.

After the Red Sea, it was Eastwards
Keeping well out of sight,
And crossing the Indian Ocean
At no time was land in our sight.

Aden was passed on our Port side
The Maldives lay somewhere ahead,
We skirted those and went further East
Where are we going, we said.

It was days before we found anything out
We slowed down, then hove to at sea,
But through the Rangefinder's powerful sights
We saw "Buy Ceylon Tea".

We had only stopped to pick up the mail
Then on our way again,
Day after day we still went East
Can't somebody please explain.

A few more days, then "Land in Sight"
A name floated round, "Singapore",
The place where my Brother, was "Serving his time"
For five long years or more.

I requested permission to leave the ship
And go as the Postman's mate,
The Captain agreed, "But not too long,
Be on Jardine steps at eight".

A quick trip by speed boat to said Jardine steps
Then a taxi across the Straits of Jahore,
As I left the car, they turned out the guard
They had not seen a red hat before.

A Sergeant R.A., looked me straight in the eye
Said "Who the bloody hell are you",
"I'm the Brother of a Gunner who's stationed here
His name is Hallas, hut two".

They took me over to a large wicker hut
It was the shortest visit yet,
Ten minutes of news, to cover four years
Ten minutes I shall never forget.

I never saw my Brother again
For "Brothers in Arms" were we,
And as I went back to my crippled ship
A prospective Jap prisoner was he.

By now the secrets were over
They now announced the next stop,
Manilla, was our next port of call
A most expensive "Tobacco Shop".

Two days we stayed, just out at sea
And one day ashore we had,
"Cat Houses", drinks and Manila cigars
And all were cheap to be had.

The next day, up anchor and on our way
Around the speakers we stood,
"The next stop is Honolulu
And three days ashore if you're good".

Brown skinned bos'ms and short straw skirts
Swinging hips, serving ice cold beer,
Visiting "Heroes" with plenty of cash
There was nothing really to fear.

We went ashore full of hope and glee
But found to our dismay,
There were fifteen Yanks to every girl
And the prices didn't match our pay.

The decent hotels were out of bounds
The "Cat Houses" packed to the door,
And the only way to talk to a girl
Was to pay for a drink for a whore.

I quickly made friends with one, Oriel King
A PFC in the Marines,
A few weeks later, he was killed by the Japs
A fresh faced kid, in his teens.

We then crossed the Equator and Dateline
With their ceremonies quite unique,
And drinking "The Potion" and swallowing "The Pill"
And things of which we don't speak.

Meanwhile, William Joyce, Known as "Lord Haw Haw"
Broadcast as cool as you please,
That the Germans had sunk the Warspite
And she'd gone down in the South China Seas.

Our loved ones must have been frantic
The rest of Britain stunned,
For the Warspite was a Jutland Vet'
That had never yet been outgunned.

We were not allowed by censor
To say where we might be,
But a newly made friend, A U.S. Marine
Wrote a letter home for me.

He didn't mention name or ship
Just Honolulu News,
But it brought peace of mind to our loved ones
And cancelled out the bad news.

The West coast of Canada soon came into sight
We slowed down and painted the ship,
With a Battleship Grey, that was almost white
We erased the scars of the trip.

We "Dressed Ship" for entering harbour
To the sound of Canadian cheers,
For we were the first British Battleship
They had seen in the past twenty years.

Gleaming light grey from stem to stern
We steamed Puget Sound with ease,
Thirty thousand tons of steel
We looked like "The Queen of the Seas".

We entered the Port of Seattle
They drowned the sirens with cheers,
For the stories of Narvik and Matapan
Had reached even their distant ears.

I had a letter to give to a girl
Outside the main gate of the Port,
The address I had, was the "Admirals Rooms"
You'll find it quite easy, he thought.

I came out of the gate, in this large place
And made my way to a Cop',
I asked him to point out "The Admirals Rooms"
I thought he was going to drop.

He explained, I had asked for a Brothel
That only opened at night,
So I gently slipped the letter in
And made it fast, out of sight.

My stay in Seattle was short and sweet
No more round "the Haunts" would I roam,
For in big black letters on the notice board,
Hallas B. was posted home.

THE BETRAYAL OF SINGAPORE

A Bastion of Far Eastern Empire
Described as "The Country's Last Ditch",
The home of Remittance Men and Planters
Bankers and sons of the rich.

There were lots of hard working Colonials
And those of the posh upper class,
Who lived a life of comfort and ease
As did the Army's Top Brass.

The Army of course could protect them
But the rank and file could not mix,
For Raffles and establishments like it
Were the playground of the rich.

Not all of the place was restricted
The Brothels, Dance Halls and Bars,
Rang up their tills with the Soldiers pay
And the cash of the visiting Tars.

But not forever would this snobbery last
For "War Talk" was well to the fore,
And soon, it would be "Tommy this and Tommy that"
As it was in the days of yore.

The Seventh Heavy Battery, out on the point
Found out to their dismay,
That their guns would only face seawards
A stupid mistake, one would say.

Those stupid mistakes by Government
Like Norway, Dunkirk and Crete,
Were explained away by the powers that be
As a strategic and planned retreat.

Eventually, some of the guns turned round
To attack an advancing foe,
But having no High Explosive Shells
The result was a bloody poor show.

Armour Piercing was all that they had
For sinking ships out at sea,
But for concentrations of enemy troops
High Explosive, it had to be.

So another mistake had come to light
Once again brave men had died,
Their Artillery was changed for rifles
But too late to stem the tide.

Given a chance and given the tools
These men could have saved the day,
But "The Keepers" of our Empire
For years had led them astray.

The Governor, who was too late with his warning
The City that was left brightly lit,
Providing a target for Japanese bombs
That succeeded with hit after hit.

It really should never have happened
The Japs were outnumbered, outclassed,
But their leaders were well trained fanatics
And unfortunately, we lived in the past.

They were ferocious, vindictive and cruel
Like animals out for the kill,
They neither asked for, nor gave any mercy
They tortured and murdered at will.

They were "Given" our Troops as prisoners
The surrender was given too soon,
For some it were better to have fought and died
Than to dance to the Japanese tune.

The Death Camps were not just at Changi
The "Railway of Death" took it's toll,
And they beat them from Java to Kokopo
And starved them to death in "The Hole".

They worked them till they were skin and bone
And those that spoke up were defiled,
Then thrown out to die in the Jungle
And be the prey for anything wild.

There's no forgiveness for treatment like this
Yet, they were not even punished by law,
And to look at their inscrutable faces
It was hard to believe what we saw.

But now their day is over
"The Rising Sun" has set,
The Prison Camps are empty
But we're not home as yet.

We took our emaciated comrades
To Columbo, St. Joseph's and bed
And not wanting to kill them with kindness
A notice, saying "Not to be Fed".

It took days to prepare them for travel
But the girls in the Forces were grand,
They treated those "Skeletons" like the heroes they were
And took them for walks, hand in hand.

They talked gently of their loved ones
Of those they had left behind,
Not a word of what they had suffered
It was all in the back of the mind.

But they will never forget, "Those Singapore Men"
The horrors and sights that they saw,
And they will never buy anything "Made in Japan"
Those "Far Eastern Prisoners of War".

IT HAPPENED ON A SUNDAY

The Parade Ground of the Royal Marine barracks is to say the least the "Holy of Holies". Every scrap of paper has been removed by hand. All of the windows visible from the square have been cleaned and polished and woe betide the man who is caught peeping out.

The Battalion is formed up in full ceremonial splendour. The Regimental Band, immaculate as always is on the left of the Battalion. Outside the Officer's Mess in the corner of the parade ground the senior officers are assembled in all their splendour.

The central figure is of course, the Adjutant, fully booted and spurred and mounted on a magnificent, usually chestnut, stallion. He is superb, it is his day and when all is ready, he orders the main gates to be opened and invites the citizens of the Town to enter and admire the spectacle.

Then it happened, entering by the guard room gate and marching across the front of the assembled Battalion, marched a bedraggled body of men in an assortment of items of clothing that had to be seen to be believed. Led by a Sergeant in khaki trousers, a duffle coat and a rather crumpled forage cap, it was not a pretty sight.

By their bearing they gave the impression that not so long ago, they too had been immaculate and gloried in the applause of the crowd. The Battle for the Island of Crete had been long and bloody, they had left behind them, comrades who would never again come home. They were weary. The glamour of the occasion left them unmoved, but they marched tall.

They were home.

THE RABBLE COMES HOME

We were remnants of our damaged ships
And we were homeward bound,
We possessed what we stood up in
Some begged, some borrowed, some found.

We changed our trains at London
Where we sometimes took over "The Guard",
But today we faced the stares of the crowd
Like something dug up in the yard.

Arriving at Chatham, our H.Q. Base
We marched in columns of threes,
It was only five minutes to the Barrack gates
Please God, let us get there please.

On the Square, the Battalion paraded
In full ceremonial blues,
Their brasses gleamed in the morning sun
And the band played softly, "The Blues".

For Sunday was the big moral day
When the Adjutant led his men,
Around the Town to the Parish Church
And then, smartly back again.

But this Sunday was certainly different
For, to the Adjutant's dismay,
A shower of scruffy, unshaven Marines
Marched in to spoil his day.

In the presence of this gleaming parade
We felt dirty, unkempt and undressed,
And sensing the importance of the occasion
Not a little depressed.

The Adjutant stretched up in his saddle
Letting forth an explicit tirade,
"I do not know who the hell you are,
But get that Rabble off the parade".

Our Sergeant stopped us in our tracks
And in a voice, so sweet,
Said, "This Rabble, Sir, are Royal Marines,
Survivors from His Majesty's Fleet".

The Townsfolk were moved, a ripple of applause
Sounded around the Square,
It was heard quite clearly at the Officers Mess
And by the Commandant standing there.

The Brigade Major, standing by his side
Was moved to take a hand,
He turned to the tall Drum Major
Requesting to call up the band.

The Band was called to attention
The Adjutant, now serene and staid,
Said "Sergeant, march off your Royal Marines,
And march them across the parade.

To the sound of the Regimental March
"A Life on the Ocean Wave",
We stretched ourselves to six foot six
And all of our best we gave.

The Battalion, the cheering Townsfolk
Were there to mark the route,
As we proudly marched past our Commandant
"The Rabble" took the salute.

CUTTER RACING, ROYAL MARINE STYLE

Cutter races were a means of creating a friendly competitive spirit between the various divisions on board H.M. Ships and on Capital ships always included the members of the Royal Marines detachment. An inclusion which in itself tended to raise the determination to be the ships champions to a deadly but always friendly fever pitch.

One Cutter was always reserved for racing. Many working hours were spent by the various crews on scraping the hull to an almost paper thin shell. Sandpapered and greased, this one boat, above all others was protected from the never ending duties of provisioning the ship, transporting liberty men and the one hundred and one other jobs required for the efficient running of the ship.

It must be obvious that in inter-departmental races, to win the toss was a great advantage, but in an inter-fleet race with other ships, the racing cutter was given to the chosen crew who were to defend the honour of that particular ship.

Such then, was the story of the cutter of H.M. Ship Warspite, in Mombasa Harbour, off the East coast of Africa in 1943.

THE ROYAL MARINES RACING CUTTER

We were anchored off the coast of Mombasa
The crew were painting ships side,
We were having a rest from "the Aussie Run"
And were anchored, Kilindini side.

For months we had been living with tension
And now we had nothing to do,
So the Commander ordered a cutter race
He said, "It will be good for the crew".

So the Topmen, Foc'sle and Quarterdeck
Old ones and some in their teens,
Trained alongside the Signals and Stokers
And of course, the Marines.

For the Royal Marines it was blood and sweat
For they were always expected to win,
So every morning, while others slept
They were getting their training in.

Now there are two cutters on every ship
For racing and provisioning with stores,
The one for provisioning is built like a tank
The racer is light, with light oars.

The Bye's and ties were soon over
The final race was on,
The Foc'sle and the Royal Marines
Will decide, which is the one.

In a three mile race, "The Racer"
Was better by five or six lengths,
But the heavy "Provisioning Cutter"
Would tax even Hercules strength.

On the day, the Marines were unlucky
They had drawn the heavy boat,
And the Foc'sle crew kept a fairly straight face
It was hard for them not to gloat.

Mombasa went quiet as the crews lined up
All tense at the starting gate,
The gun was fired, we strained at the oars
To a well timed twenty eight.

After two miles we were neck and neck
Out "Tank" was holding it's own,
But slowly, ever so slowly
The "Racer" went forward alone.

On top of the Warspite's turret
The Major, could see his crew's plight,
That the weight of the heaviest Cutter
Was taxing even their might.

He changed the beat to thirty
The Drummer increased the time,
And we in the boat strained our hearts out
To reach that finishing line.

The "Racer's" crew were now hard put
Some extra strength to find,
And the Royal Marines just crossed the line
A bare half length behind.

Meanwhile the Resolution
Had timed the winning boat,
And knowing that their time was faster
Sat back with a bit of a gloat.

They sent a challenge with five hundred pounds
And challenged the Warspite's boat,
And please, "Would the Warspite cover it"
Said the rather demanding note.

The Captain asked the Foc'sle crew
As the champions of the ship,
If they would take on the Reso'
And stop them from giving their lip.

The Foc'sle crew thought long and hard,
And then said as one man,
"Sir, if we had had the provisioning boat
We'd have been an also ran".

"So please accept the Reso's bet
And cover it note for note,
But let "The Royals" take up the glove
And give them "The Racing Boat".

We will not give up the championship
But, for the honour of the ship,
Just this once we'll all stand down
And the Royals can make the trip.

So the day of the challenge came round at last
The crews lined up at the flag,
"We'll tan the arse off the Flagship's boat"
The Resolution began to brag.

But then, they saw our colours
The yellow, green, red and blue,
"We're not racing the Foc'sle boat", they said
"It's a bloody Bootnecks crew".

The gun fired, we all strained backwards
The beat, was again twenty eight,
It didn't take half of the three mile course
For the Reso' to work out their fate.

Ten lengths ahead on the finishing line
The Reso's crew truly beat,
And to rub it in, on the Warspite's mast
They were flying "The Cock of the Fleet".

They towed our boat back to the Warspite
To the Major, containing his pride,
The Foc'sle crew came and shook our hands
"It was nothing" we said "We just tried".

That night we went to the Naval Canteen
Each man had to stand a round,
And thirteen bottles is a hell of a load
To keep your feet on the ground.

Our rival Marines on the Reso'
Just to join in the fun,
Invited us back to their Sergeant's Mess
To make a hole in their rum.

We came back to the ship quite legless
All this because of a bet,
And not able to walk up the gangway
They hauled us aboard in a net.

The Officer of the Watch was astounded
"My God, what have we here,
A net full of drunken Royal Marines,
It's Commander's report I fear".

But the Major, brought down from the Wardroom Mess
Turned out really "True Blue",
He said, "Scrub out the charge, and put them to bed,
They're my Racing Cutters Crew".

SALERNO, ITALY – 1943

We had flown our Flag all over the World
For the war had caused us to roam,
But now things were better, or so it would seem
And we were on our way home.

The heights of Spain lay to starboard
Morocco stood off our port beam,
Once we were clear of the Straits of Gib
We were home, our one and only dream.

But before we were clear, high up in the sky
An Aldis Lamp flashes like mad,
A Catalina was transmitting in code
We guessed that the news would be bad.

The words "Hard to Port" were passed to the wheel
"Hard to Port" the wheelhouse replied,
We turned half circle and made our way back
To a man, we bloody near died.

The Tannoy crackled, "This is your Captain" it said
"You'll have guessed what it's all about,
Our Forces on land are in a bit of a fix
And we're going to help them out".

Soon Sicily was way astern
And Salerno lay ahead,
The harbour was jammed with Landing Craft
A fix is right, we said.

The Germans were holding the high ground
The passes too, they controlled,
The only way to dislodge them
Was to do something really quite bold.

So, the Warspite entered the harbour
And bombarded the enemy tanks,
We plastered the heights and North of the Pass
And cleared a way for the Yanks.

The American 5th Army went forward
British Commandos took care of the Pass,
For the moment the danger was over
We were now advancing, en mass.

Suddenly, as of old, "Aircraft Red" was the cry
Three planes came out of the sun,
The centre plane was really a bomb
In that harbour, no way could we run.

The bomb hit us almost amidships
The damage was bad we could tell,
For the water rushed in and we listed
Our steering had gone as well.

We had always been the victor
Except for that one day at Crete,
And to be at the enemy's mercy
Was really not up our street.

Every submergible pump was in use
And parties were baling below,
With fear in our minds, but not in our hearts
Thinking, this is no way to go.

We manned our guns but dare not fire
The list we had was severe,
What would happen when the Bombers came
Was our one and only fear.

Two American tugs were struggling
To keep us on the go,
Our lights were out, we worked in the dark
But to our stern there showed a faint glow.

The enemy Bombers saw the glow
And came in for the kill,
But what they found was a fighting ship
That didn't quite fit their bill.

When the dawn came, the Bombers withdrew
No damage had they done,
For the glow astern was the Valiant
Showing lights to lead them on.

For, seeing her "Sistership" crippled
She had swung astern in our wake,
And steaming along with her lights switched on
She had taken what we couldn't take.

The Straits of Messina were dead ahead
We were swinging into the rough,
The American tugs were doing their best
But it seemed it was not enough.

Then as the morning sun rose high
And the sea mist disappeared,
The Orion and the Nimble
Two London tugs appeared.

With expertise they cast their lines
The hawsers took the strain,
And thanking the Americans for their help
We were picking up speed again.

No water, no sleep, with a five day beard
And the Island of Malta in sight,
We relaxed and took our second breath
It appeared everything now was just right.

Our berth was prepared, we were towed into place
The hawsers screamed their protest,
But they held her fast to the side of the dock
Where she shuddered and then came to rest.

Every ship in the harbour was now "Sounding Off"
The Maltese, first cheered, then cried,
For rumour had spread all over the Isle
That the veteran "Old Lady" had died.

The Captain thanked us all "For bringing her home"
We thanked him in return, "For the ride",
Then he ordered the Bugler to sound off "Secure"
And we dropped where we could and just "Died".

NELSON'S BLOOD – THE RUM RATION

Seven Bells, and hark, the bugle sounds
Rum ration for most of the crew,
For those that declined on various grounds
Three pence a day is their due.

A Corporal in the Royal Marines
With the Officer of the day,
Proceeds to the Royal Marine Sentry
In whose care the keg and key lay.

Off to the Spirit Room two decks down
In single file they go,
The Officer, the Corporal
And the duty R.P.O.

The measure of neat spirit
So very carefully done,
Is carried aloft to the upper deck
By the side of the Four Inch gun.

Chiefs and Petty Officers
And Sergeants, Royal Marines,
Drink their ration in pure neat rum
That could take you apart at the seams.

After which it is carefully watered down
To a ratio of two to one,
And in answer to the "Lower Deck Lawyers"
The two, is water, my son.

Then each cook of the Mess draws his ration
And carries it carefully below,
Where the number of those entitled
Have their cups laid out in a row.

There's a proper routine for sharing it out
Each cup must be the same size,
And each measure must be truly exact
To cheat would not really be wise.

For rum is the currency of the lower deck
It's value can not be surpassed,
Change of watch, leave ashore, or your laundry
The rules are laid down hard and fast.

Sniffers are first, then sippers
Gulpers are next in the line,
The whole of the tot is for murder
Or at least something near to that line.

After the issue was over
The Officer inspected the tub,
What was over must be destroyed
And that was really the rub.

In their cruel and infinite wisdom
My Lords of Admiralty spake,
"You must now find the nearest scupper
And to it the surplus rum take".

The Rum Tub was slowly tilted
"The Life Blood" drained away,
There were tears as it flowed down the scupper
The Officer, saluted and then marched away.

But the crafty Corporal of Royal Marines
With the precision of a job often done,
Bent down and retrieved a tobacco tin
Filled to the brim with rum.

This tin's always kept in the scupper
And kept clean, "Under threat of Death",
Woe betide the person that fouls it
He would most certainly draw his last breath.

But that was all in yesteryear
The years they say were the best,
The years of the really true Mataloe
With hairs upon his chest.

Now to look at today's bright Sailors
With faces and skin like silk,
You can only blame it on the lack of rum
Replaced with "Cola and Milk".

THE OLD LADY – H.M.S. WARSPITE

Noblesse oblige, no other choice remained
Pay homage, therefore, ye who pass her by,
Last of a line of Royal Ancestry
Whose roots were struck when Gloriana reigned.

For well nigh three decades from sea to sea
Remained she faithful in the hour of need,
To all the best traditions of her breed
The breakers yard no tomb for such as she.

Young in her heart, men saw her born anew
What time the name affection bred was won,
An ancient dame who showed she still could run
And teach the young ideas a thing or two.

She craves no pity, makes no plaint or boast
Then leave her, rock and seaweed for her bed,
In peace until the sea gives up it's dead
Soothed by the waves that wash her Island's coast.

And when your children gather round your knee
And ask her story, tell them,
"It was hers to win the love of countless Mariners,
By what she was, and taught them too, to be".

Admiral Ronald Hopwood C.B.

THE SUBJECT

You say you have no subject
And your brushes all have dried,
Then come ye to Marazion
At the ebbing of the tide.

And look you out to seaward
Where my Lady battle scarred,
Hugs the rocks that are more welcome
Than the shameful breakers yard.

Paint her there upon the Sunset
In her glory and despair,
With the diadem of Victory
Still in flower upon her hair.

Let her whisper as she settles
Of her blooding long ago,
In the mist that mingles Jutland
With the might of Scapa Flow.

Let her tell you of Narvik
With it's snowy hills, and then,
Of Matapan, Salerno
And the shoals of Walcheren.

And finally of Malta
When along the purple street,
Came in trail the Roman Navy
To surrender at her feet.

Of all these honours conscious
How could she bear to be,
Delivered to the spoiler
Or severed from the sea.

So hasten then and paint her
In the last flush of her pride,
On the rocks, just off Marazion
At the ebbing of the tide.

By Lieutenant Commander A.B. Mitchell
H.M.S. Warspite 1939-1942

AT PEACE WITH THE WORLD

I have had my fill of death and hate
No more the seas will I roam,
The smell of Cordite has vanished for good
And now it's the smell of home.

A home that is now secure from the threat
Of a madman incensed with hate,
Who cost us tears, and blood and sweat
But the end was well worth the wait.

Admittedly the price was high
Our friends buried far and wide,
We can only honour their memory
And remember for what they had died.

So now it's peace and all hands to the wheel,
And let's get on with the task,
Of creating a World that's fit for us all
I think that's all they would ask.

Then looking forward to a World of equals
Marching forward, with flags unfurled,
Millions of loving families,
Creating a better World.

So I've put away my guns and shells
And settled down in my chair,
With my loved ones thankfully by my side
Sans Youth, sans Teeth, sans Hair.

WHAT IS IT?

What is it to be so "Young in Heart"
To feel as you did in the past,
To ignore all aches and feel no pain
With the wrinkles smoothed out at last.

What is it that helps the months go by
While ignoring the rain and the cold,
With you and your loved one hand in hand
Looking forward to days of gold.

What is it that makes you scrimp and save
To spend some time in the sun,
Take off your clothes, develop a tan
Forget work and join in the fun.

What is it that drives you on and on
To seek new fields afar,
To drive, to sail, to walk for miles
Seeking that bright new "Spa".

What is it to be so happy and gay
Thanking God that you have been born,
To smile and nod, to all that you meet
And dance away 'til the dawn.

And then when it's over, the strength all gone
And you feel like an also ran,
You stop and charge your batteries again
With the love of your fellow man.

THE THATCHER YEARS

Thatcherism was not just a word
It was more of a way of life,
It controlled the standards of the people it ruled
Setting class against class, with an increase in strife.

Ten years or more she had held the wheel
It had not been a steady course,
There had been many troughs and breakers to face
But she had sailed on with unbreakable force.

Of mutineers she had had her share
There were others just waiting to board,
Her First Lieutenants were jostling to cut
The thread holding Damocles Sword.

Her voice was tuned to suit any debate
It could cut through the House like a knife,
At times it was dulcet like gossamer wings
At others, like a Fishmonger's Wife.

The rest of the World acclaimed and admired
Whilst at home there were those that cursed,
She endured both sides, taking fame and scorn
With head erect and soft lips pursed.

Some say she had divided the Nation
And with contempt had ignored the poor,
But one thing at least was certainly true
For those that got less, there were others that got more.

The control of this Country's great assets
Were transferred from the most to the few,
The few that controlled the purse strings
And whose wealth just grew and grew.

Matters were bound to come to a head
The murmurs had grown to a roar,
Her crew were divided and not without cause
For their standing had never been lower.

She had tried sleight of hand and reshuffled the pack
And kept her feet "Clear of the Rug",
Some followers had tried to support her in vain
But the majority had pulled out the plug.

The conniving, the jibes, the whispers
Wrote "Fini" to the end of the show,
For now at last the curtain was down
And "Maggie" had had to go.

She is still out there in the shadows
Her voice is heard now and then,
And if ever her crew were to founder her ship
Would she come back, and if so, when.

U.F.O.'s

Somewhere deep in the velvet void
The U.F.O's cruise around,
Hiding behind the scudding clouds
Determined not to be found.

A fleeting glimpse of flickering light
A hint of vapour trail,
Disguising themselves as a shooting star
Or a Comet without a tail.

They hover at night over country lanes
When the countryside is asleep,
Observed by the lonely traveller
And the ever present sheep.

Are they stocking their larders
Even Aliens we suppose, must eat,
Or, are they seeking contact
Perhaps one day we shall meet.

And on that day we shall realise
As their minds control our will,
That we, the denizens of Earth
Have merely been standing still.

(C)   Bernard Hallas

OUR MEN OF THE SEA

The cobbled streets of Humberside
No longer reek of fish
The wiles and use of Spanish guile
Killed off our national dish.

With faces long and tempers short
And failing to comprehend,
The "Fishermen of England"
Have only this message to send.

We who fly the "Red Duster"
Deserve far more than this,
Unarmed, we faced the "U" Boats
To feed our nation with fish

It was we who heard the ancient call
Of Sir Francis Drake and his "Drum",
As our Armies lay exhausted in France
Over run by the speeding Hun.

Our fishing boats and trawlers
Sped to the enemy coast,
"Dunkirk" is a name to remember
And a deed of which we can boast.

But now the war is over
And we still have a nation to feed,
So give us the means to rebuild our Fleet
And to compete with Europe's greed.

Then we, "The Fishermen of England"
Can sail once again on the tide,
Braving once again the elements
And flying "Our Flag" with pride.

Bernard Hallas
Ex-Royal Marines (1935-1947)
Haxby, York.

LOOK BACK IN ANGER

What can we say of our prowess
Or of the leaders that we thought we had,
Of the stupid ideas that they nurtured
And their decisions we all thought were mad.

The expedition to save Norway
Was fated right from the start,
The troops were untrained and ill equipped
And unable to play their part.

Followed too soon by the B.E.F.
With their leaders outdated for war
The sands that were soon to be known as "Dunkirk"
Were the bloodiest that the world ever saw.

Dieppe was a Churchillian rehearsal
He was testing the enemy's might,
Another four thousand were lost to the cause
And his cohorts still said he was right.

Arnhem was another mistake
Four thousand more were dead,
They tried to blame their radios
And a "Bridge too Far" they said.

A different war, a different clime
To relieve the town of Torbruk,
A complete "Commando" was blown to shreds
And not just a case of bad luck.

The leaders in their bunkers
Were too far away from the fight,
They could not agree with the men on the spot
And still they thought they were right.

Crete, was now the biggest blunder of all
We had to admit defeat,
Twenty Six Warships were blown to hell
And almost two thousand deaths in the Fleet.

It could never happen in Singapore
With sixty four thousand armed men,
But it seemed once again, they had made a mistake
It was abandoned with the stroke of a pen.

The Mountbattens, the Churchills, the Wavells
Can deny the mistakes that they made,
But we who were left to carry on
Must thank the world who came to our aid.

The war is long over, we can mourn our dead
Buried so far and wide,
And the few who created the chaos
Have their Statues and Titles,
But no pride.

Bernard Hallas
Ex-Royal Marines (1935-1947)
Haxby, York.